CODE MONKEYS

Using Technology

BY JOHN WOOD

BookLife
PUBLISHING

©2020
BookLife Publishing Ltd.
King's Lynn
Norfolk PE30 4LS

A catalogue record for this book is available from the British Library.

ISBN: 978-1-83927-115-1

Written by:
John Wood

Edited by:
Robin Twiddy

Designed by:
Danielle Webster-Jones

IMAGE CREDITS

Contents

Words that look like **this** can be found in the glossary on page 24.

Welcome
TO THE JUNGLE

A code monkey is a curious, clever little thing. It wants to know all about computers and coding. Let's follow the code monkeys and learn about coding too!

No! Bad code monkey! Bring back those wires!

FIRST THINGS FIRST

COMPUTER

a machine that can carry out **instructions**

CODING

writing a set of instructions, called code, to tell computers what to do

PROGRAMMER

a person who writes code (like a human code monkey)

Computers are everywhere. Desktops, laptops, smartphones and tablets are all computers. There are even computers in surprising places, from fridges to lampposts.

Coding
IN THE WILD

Look! It's a smart TV. But how do smart TVs know when to change the channel? How do they know when to record your programmes? Well, it is because some clever programmers told them how to do it.

Someone had to write the code to make all of these things work. Without programmers, these computers wouldn't know what to do.

All sorts of things can have computers inside them, such as cars, microwaves and toys.

INPUTS AND OUTPUTS

A computer is made up of lots of different parts. Some of these parts take in **information** – these are called inputs. Some of these parts give out information – these are called outputs.

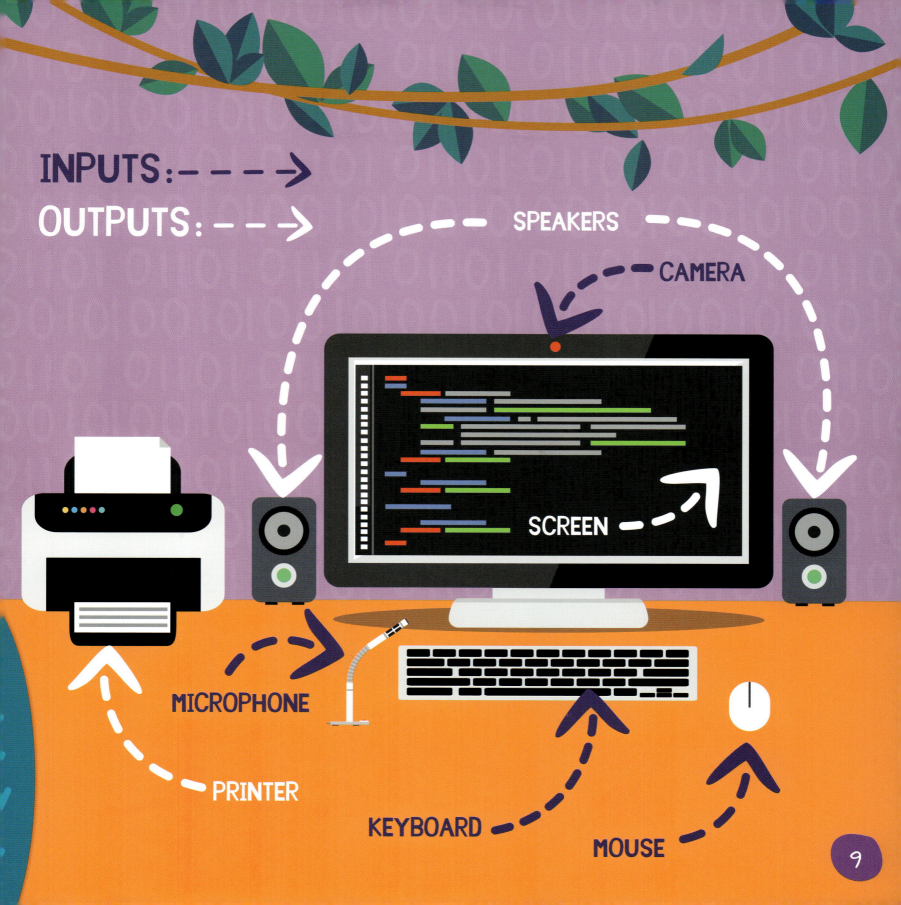

Hardware AND Software

The things that make up a computer can be sorted into two groups: hardware and software.

Hardware is the stuff you can touch, such as the keyboard and mouse. You can find lots of hardware inside a computer too.

FAN
Fans keep inside the computer cool.

The parts of a computer that you can't touch are called software. For example, you can't touch an **app** on a smartphone, so it is software. Software is built from code.

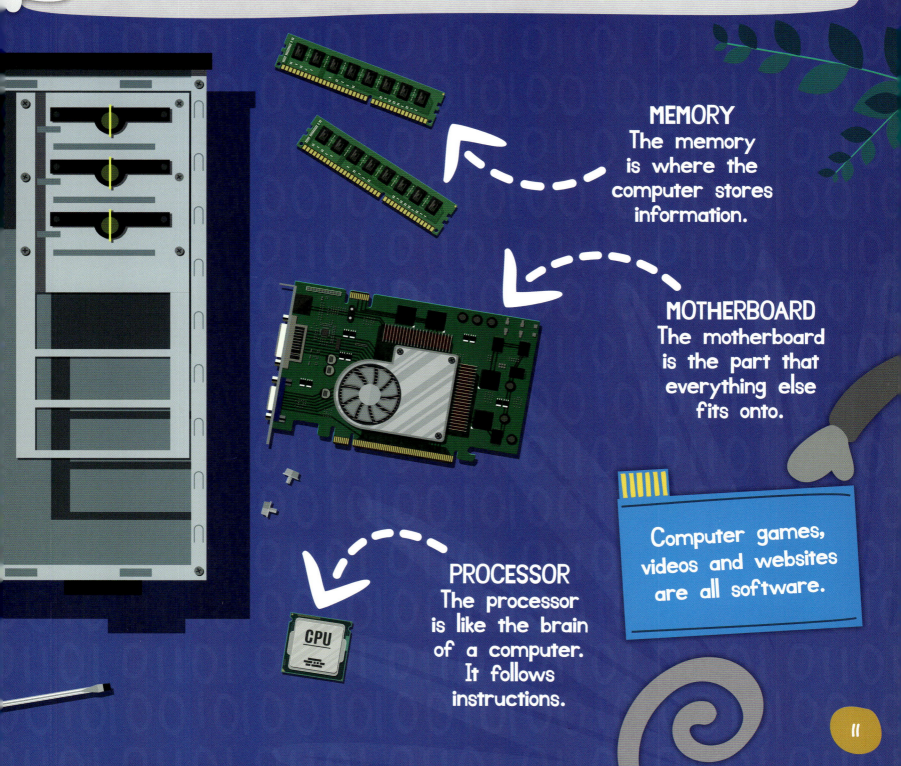

MEMORY
The memory is where the computer stores information.

MOTHERBOARD
The motherboard is the part that everything else fits onto.

PROCESSOR
The processor is like the brain of a computer. It follows instructions.

Computer games, videos and websites are all software.

1s AND 0s

Computers speak a strange language called binary. Binary is made out of 1s and 0s. When these 1s and 0s are put in a certain order, they make up a language that a computer understands.

The **circuits** of a computer are made up of lots of **transistors**. 1s mean a transistor is turned on, while 0s mean the transistor is turned off.

> 0001110110
> 001000110101
> 0101010011
> 00110101

> ooh ooh ah ah
> ooh ooh ah ah
> ooh ooh ah ah
> ooh ooh ah ah

Binary is very difficult for humans (and code monkeys) to understand. Look below to find out how to count in binary, and how to say the first three letters of the alphabet.

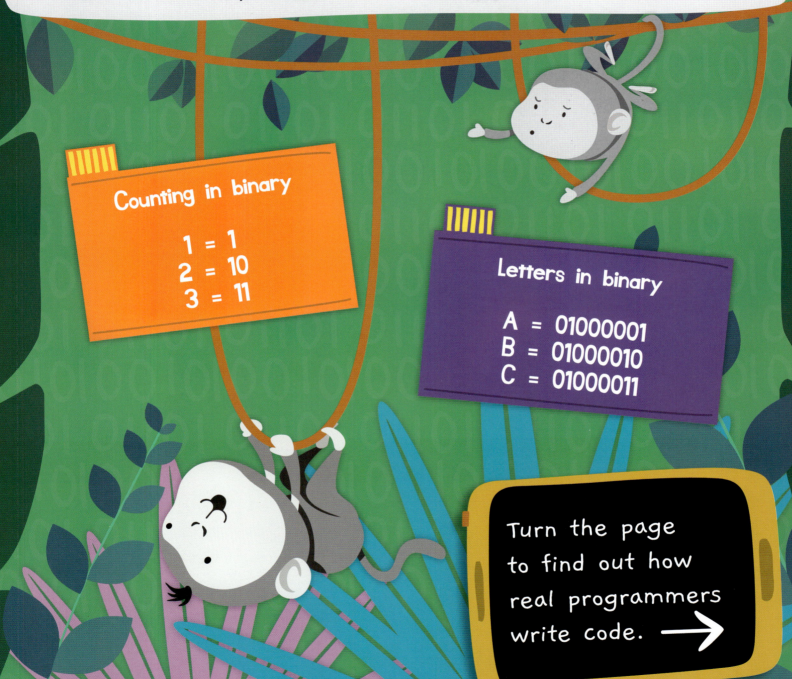

Counting in binary

1 = 1
2 = 10
3 = 11

Letters in binary

A = 01000001
B = 01000010
C = 01000011

Turn the page to find out how real programmers write code. →

TALKING IN Code

Programmers write code in special languages called programming languages. These are easier for humans to understand and they can be translated into binary afterwards.

All programming languages have different rules on how they are written. Each language uses different words and <u>symbols</u>.

There are lots of different programming languages. They are all good at different things.

HTML, CSS and JavaScript are great for making websites.

C++ is good for big, **complicated** games.

Python is a good programming language for making apps.

Scratch is a good programming language to learn how coding works. It uses simple blocks of instructions that snap together.

SECRET MONKEYS

It is important to stay safe on the internet. You can stay safe by not giving away too much information about yourself. People may not be who they say they are on the internet.

Do not give out your address or your phone number on the internet. Think carefully when putting pictures of yourself online.

Always bring an adult with you if you are meeting someone you've only talked to online.

It is also important to keep your passwords secret. Your password should be a mix of numbers, letters and symbols. It should be easy for you to remember, but hard for other people to guess.

Don't write your passwords down. Keep them in your head!

Climb TO SAFETY

The internet is great, and we can use it for lots of things. However, sometimes the internet isn't so great. You might see things you don't like or that you don't understand.

Some parts of the internet are not safe for children. You should talk to an adult about which websites are safe.

18

If you see something that upsets you or something that you don't understand, you should leave the computer straight away. Go and talk to an adult you trust, and they will help you.

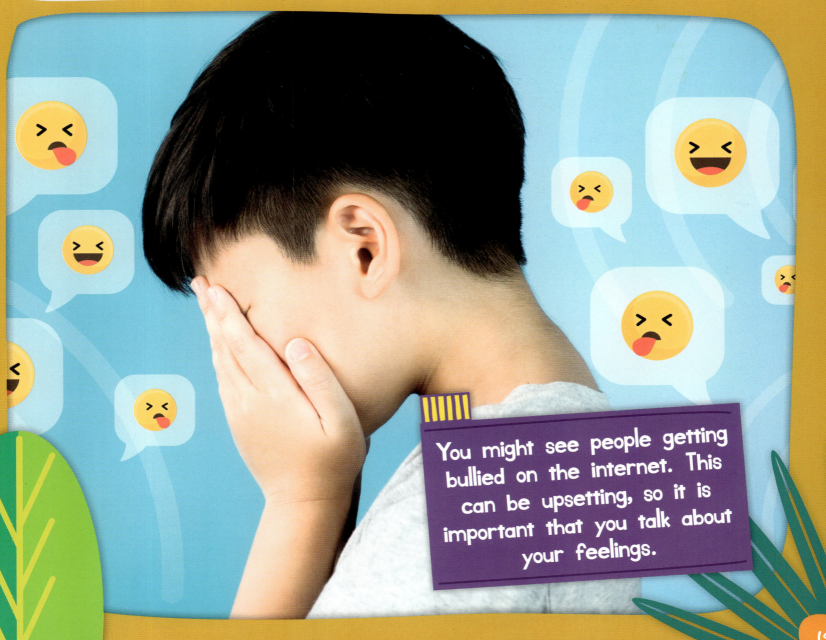

You might see people getting bullied on the internet. This can be upsetting, so it is important that you talk about your feelings.

Monkey See

In the future, all the machines and **devices** around us will become more and more connected. One day, our fridges, laptops, cars and phones will all **communicate** with each other.

This idea is called the Internet of Things.

Just imagine – in the future, cars will be able to drive themselves. They will all communicate with each other so they can drive safely on the road.

A smart fridge will be able to tell the computer to order more food when there is none left.

MORE FOOD

Monkey Do

It is time to practise your **privacy** skills. Can you come up with a list of ways to stay safe on the internet? Try to come up with three to five things.

1.

2.

3.

Code monkeys always have the best passwords – now it is your turn. Try to come up with the perfect password.

Remember – the password should be easy to remember but hard to guess.

23

Glossary

app	a program that works on a mobile device, such as a smartphone
circuits	paths for electric currents to move around
communicate	to pass information between two or more things
complicated	made of many different parts and therefore hard to understand
devices	machines or inventions made to do something
information	numbers and facts that tell humans and computers about the world and the things in it
instructions	a set of steps that explain how something is done
privacy	to do with personal things that are not meant for everyone to see or know about
symbols	things that are used as a sign of something else
transistors	tiny devices used in computers to change electrical signals

Index